NZ, Canada, US and UK readers
Please note that Australian cup and spoon
measurements are metric. A quick conversion
guide appears on page 63.

how to lose weight

Eat low-fat food and get plenty of exercise – it's as simple as that. Or almost – you should eat a balanced diet and avoid Hollywood food fads. As you'll see from this book, low-fat need not be boring or tasteless.

fruit

- Fruit is a great in-between-meal snack, it is full of fibre, and much healthier than a sweet biscuit, piece of cake or chocolate bar.
- Make sure you eat a variety of fruits, so that you don't get bored and start snacking on high-fat foods.
- If eating out, have a piece of fruit one to two hours before leaving, so you aren't starving when it's time to order.

water

- Drink plenty of water. Among other things, water aids digestion, eliminates toxins and promotes clear skin. It is necessary for the health of every cell in the body.
- Often, when you think you are hungry, you could actually be thirsty. So, before reaching for that not-so-healthy snack, reach for a glass of water.
- Most of us need to drink at least eight glasses of fluid per day, more during hot days or if exercising regularly.

breakfast

- A good breakfast increases your metabolic rate, so you burn more kilojoules during the day. (However, your metabolic rate slows during the evening, so a small, light meal is best eaten at night.)
- People who eat breakfast have more stamina throughout the day, and are able to concentrate better.
- Breakfast is often the lowest fat meal of the day, and is usually a good source of fibre. Eating a high-fibre breakfast can stop those mid-morning hunger pangs.
- If you don't have time to eat at home, or you don't feel like eating in the morning, grab a cereal bar or piece of fruit to eat at work, or try something light, such as yogurt, fruit or a smoothie.

exercise

With today's hectic lifestyle, many of us don't have the time to, or, more truthfully, can't bear the thought of, going to the gym. However, there are many small ways in which you can make a big difference to your fitness level.

incidental exercise

- Walk up stairs instead of taking the lifts or escalators.
- When shopping, park your car at the far end of the car park and walk to the shops. If possible, carry your grocery bags back to the car.
- Get off the bus or train one stop earlier on the way to and from work.
- Turn housework into a workout. Burn extra kilojoules by putting on some dance music and vacuuming with vigour, or lunge while hanging out the laundry.
- Don't eat while watching TV, exercise instead. During the ad breaks, do some sit-ups or march on the spot, etc. Even better, invest in a stationary bike or treadmill and exercise during your favourite half-hour show.
- Rather than using a grass catcher on your lawn mower, rake up the grass clippings instead.
- Gardening is not only an enjoyable outdoors activity, it also can help burn off kilojoules.

general tips

- Approach your new eating and exercise habits positively. Don't think of it as hard work as this will lead to failure. A healthier lifestyle means more energy and better self esteem.
- Don't become fixated on the bathroom scales – looser clothing also indicates weight loss.
- Be realistic in your expectations. Taking off excess weight, and keeping it off, is a slow process. You have to change both your eating habits and daily routine.
- Start slowly and change just one thing at a time. For example, have a piece of fruit instead of a biscuit or chocolate bar for afternoon tea. Do this for a week, until you are comfortable with it, before you change anything else.
- Make small goals, and reward yourself after reaching each one. This will boost your confidence, and encourage you to continue with your new healthy lifestyle.

Drink at least eight glasses of water a day.

chicken summer rolls

1 medium carrot (120g)

2 green onions

1 medium red
   capsicum (200g)

2 teaspoons peanut oil

500g chicken mince

2 tablespoons
   palm sugar

2 kaffir lime leaves,
   shredded

1 tablespoon lime juice

1 teaspoon fish sauce

1 tablespoon
   sweet chilli sauce

2 tablespoons
   chicken stock

30 rice paper sheets

fresh mint leaves

fresh coriander leaves

dipping sauce

1 lebanese cucumber
   (130g), chopped finely

2 tablespoons
   sweet chilli sauce

½ cup (125ml)
   cider vinegar

2 teaspoons sugar

Cut carrot and onions into very thin, 8cm-long strips. Halve capsicum; remove and discard seeds and membranes. Slice capsicum into very thin 8cm-long strips.

Heat oil in medium frying pan; cook chicken, stirring, until browned all over. Add sugar, lime leaves, juice, sauces and stock; cook, stirring, until sugar is dissolved, cool.

Place one sheet of rice paper in medium bowl of warm water until just softened; lift from water carefully, place on board.

Place one mint leaf and one coriander leaf in centre of rice paper; top with 1 level tablespoon cooled mince mixture and a few strips of carrot, onion and capsicum. Roll to enclose, folding in ends (rolls should be about 8cm long).

Repeat with remaining rice paper sheets, mint, coriander and filling. Serve with dipping sauce.

dipping sauce Combine all ingredients in a small bowl.

makes 30

per roll 1.8g fat; 205kJ (49 cal)

vietnamese chicken salad

This dish, known as ga xe phai, is one of Vietnam's most popular salads. You need to purchase one small chinese cabbage, as well as a large barbecue chicken weighing approximately 900g for this recipe.

100g snow peas, trimmed
4 cups (400g) shredded chicken
4 cups (320g) finely shredded chinese cabbage
4 garlic chives, chopped finely
1 medium red onion (170g), sliced thinly
½ cup coarsely chopped fresh mint
1 teaspoon sambal oelek
1 teaspoon sesame oil
⅓ cup (80ml) lime juice
⅓ cup (80ml) fish sauce
2 teaspoons sugar
½ cup loosely packed fresh coriander leaves

Place snow peas in medium bowl. Cover with boiling water; drain immediately. Cover snow peas with cold water in same bowl; stand 2 minutes. Drain; slice thinly.
Combine snow peas in large bowl with chicken, cabbage, chives, onion and mint.
Combine sambal oelek, oil, juice, sauce and sugar in screw-top jar; shake well. Drizzle salad with chilli lime dressing; toss gently to combine then sprinkle coriander over salad.

serves 4
per serving 8.5g fat; 928kJ (222 cal)

chicken tandoori pockets with raita

1 tablespoon lime juice
⅓ cup (100g) tandoori paste
¼ cup (70g) low-fat yogurt
400g chicken tenderloins
8 large flour tortillas
60g snow pea tendrills
raita
1 cup (280g) low-fat yogurt
1 lebanese cucumber (130g), halved, seeded, chopped finely
1 tablespoon finely chopped fresh mint

Combine juice, paste and yogurt in medium bowl; add chicken, toss to coat chicken in marinade.
Cook chicken, in batches, on heated oiled grill plate (or grill or barbecue) until cooked through. Stand 5 minutes; slice thickly.
Meanwhile, heat tortillas according to manufacturer's instructions.
Place equal amounts of each of the chicken, tendrils and raita on a quarter section of each tortilla; fold tortilla in half and then in half again to enclose filling and form triangle-shaped pockets.
raita Combine ingredients in small bowl.

makes 8
per pocket 8.2g fat; 991kJ (237 cal)

thai chicken in lettuce-leaf cups

You need to purchase a large barbecue chicken weighing approximately 900g for this recipe.

8 large iceberg lettuce leaves
1 tablespoon kecap manis
1 teaspoon sesame oil
1 tablespoon lime juice
1 large zucchini (150g), grated coarsely
1 medium carrot (120g), grated coarsely
2 green onions, sliced thinly
1 medium red capsicum (200g), sliced thinly
4 cups (400g) shredded chicken
1 tablespoon finely chopped fresh mint
2 tablespoons coarsely chopped fresh coriander
2 tablespoons sweet chilli sauce

Trim lettuce-leaf edges with scissors. Place leaves in large bowl of iced water; refrigerate.
Meanwhile, combine kecap manis, oil and juice in large bowl. Add zucchini, carrot, onion, capsicum, chicken, mint and half of the coriander; toss gently to combine.
Dry lettuce; divide leaves among serving plates. Top with chicken mixture; drizzle with combined sweet chilli sauce and remaining coriander.

serves 4
per serving 8.8g fat; 903kJ (216 cal)

chicken, vegetable and rice noodle stir-fry

500g fresh wide rice noodles
1 teaspoon sesame oil
500g chicken breast fillets, sliced thinly
250g oyster mushrooms, sliced thinly
¼ cup (60ml) oyster sauce
1 tablespoon fish sauce
1 tablespoon sugar
2 teaspoons sambal oelek
250g baby spinach leaves
¼ cup coarsely chopped fresh coriander

Rinse noodles in strainer under hot water. Separate noodles with fork; drain.
Meanwhile, heat oil in wok or large frying pan; stir-fry chicken, in batches, until browned all over and cooked through.
Place mushrooms in wok; stir-fry until just tender. Return chicken to wok with noodles, sauces, sugar and sambal oelek; stir-fry until heated through.
Remove from heat. Add baby spinach and coriander; toss gently to combine.

serves 4
per serving 5.6g fat; 1885kJ (451 cal)

pepper-grilled lamb fillets with roasted root vegetables

All manner of baby vegetables are available at better greengrocers and some supermarkets. You could also serve baby cauliflower, baby turnips and baby pumpkin with the lamb in this recipe.

1kg baby beetroots, trimmed
6 small parsnips (360g), quartered
500g baby new potatoes, halved
400g baby carrots, trimmed
8 baby onions (200g), halved
4 cloves garlic, peeled
¼ cup (60ml) orange juice
¼ cup (90g) honey
1 tablespoon wholegrain mustard
12 lamb fillets (960g)
1½ tablespoons cracked black pepper

Preheat oven to moderately hot.
Boil, steam or microwave unpeeled beetroot until tender; drain. When cool enough to handle, peel beetroot.
Combine beetroot in large lightly oiled baking dish with parsnip, potato, carrot, onion and garlic. Pour combined juice, honey and mustard over vegetables; roast, uncovered, in moderately hot oven, stirring occasionally, about 45 minutes or until vegetables are browned and tender.
Meanwhile, coat lamb all over with pepper. Cook lamb on heated oiled grill plate (or grill or barbecue) until browned all over and cooked as desired. Cover; stand 10 minutes. Slice thickly.
Serve vegetables topped with lamb.

serves 8
per serving 4.8g fat; 1229kJ (294 cal)

lamb chermoulla with chickpea salad

Chermoulla is a Moroccan mixture of fresh and ground spices including coriander, cumin and paprika. It can be used as a marinade for chicken, meat and fish.

300g green beans, trimmed
2 teaspoons cracked
　black pepper
2 teaspoons ground cumin
2 teaspoons ground
　coriander
1 teaspoon hot paprika
2 tablespoons coarsely
　chopped fresh
　flat-leaf parsley
2 tablespoons coarsely
　chopped fresh
　coriander leaves
2 tablespoons coarsely
　chopped fresh
　mint leaves
1 tablespoon coarsely
　grated lemon rind
¼ cup (60ml) water
1 medium red onion
　(170g), chopped finely
8 lamb fillets (700g)
400g can brown lentils,
　rinsed, drained
300g can chickpeas,
　rinsed, drained
⅓ cup coarsely
　chopped fresh
　flat-leaf parsley, extra
2 cloves garlic, crushed
2 tablespoons lemon juice

Cut beans into 3cm lengths; boil, steam or microwave beans until just tender. Refresh under cold water; drain.

Blend or process pepper, spices, herbs, rind, the water and half of the onion until mixture forms a paste.

Coat lamb with chermoulla paste in large bowl; cook, in batches, on heated oiled grill plate (or grill or barbecue) until browned and cooked as desired. Cover; stand 5 minutes before slicing thickly.

Combine beans, lentils, chickpeas, extra parsley, garlic and juice with remaining onion in large bowl; toss gently to combine. Serve chickpea salad with lamb.

serves 4
per serving 8.3g fat; 1373kJ (328 cal)
tip The salad can be assembled several hours ahead; add juice just before serving.

satay beef and stir-fried vegetables with rice

1 litre (4 cups) water

1 cup (200g) basmati rice

1 teaspoon peanut oil

500g lean beef topside, sliced thinly

1 large brown onion (200g), sliced thinly

1 clove garlic, crushed

2cm piece fresh ginger (10g), grated finely

2 small fresh red thai chillies, seeded, chopped finely

1 medium red capsicum (200g), chopped coarsely

1 medium green capsicum (200g), chopped coarsely

100g button mushrooms, halved

225g can bamboo shoots, drained

1 teaspoon curry powder

2 teaspoons cornflour

½ cup (125ml) chicken stock

¼ cup (70g) light smooth peanut butter

2 tablespoons oyster sauce

1 tablespoon unsalted, roasted, coarsely chopped peanuts

Bring the water to a boil in large saucepan; stir in rice. Boil, uncovered, about 15 minutes or until rice is just tender. Drain, rinse under hot water; drain rice again, cover to keep warm.

Meanwhile, heat oil in wok or large non-stick frying pan; stir-fry beef, in batches, until browned all over.

Reheat meat juices in wok; stir-fry onion and garlic until onion softens.

Add ginger, chilli, capsicums, mushrooms, bamboo shoots and curry powder; stir-fry until vegetables are just tender.

Blend cornflour with stock in small jug; pour into wok, stir to combine with vegetable mixture. Return beef to wok with peanut butter and oyster sauce; bring to a boil. Boil, stirring, until sauce thickens slightly, and beef is cooked as desired. Sprinkle with peanuts; serve with rice.

serves 4

per serving 14g fat; 2383kJ (570 cal)

tip Use sliced lamb fillets or sliced chicken thigh fillets instead of the beef, if you prefer.

thai beef salad

You'll need to buy one bunch of fresh thai basil, two bunches of fresh coriander, one bunch of fresh vietnamese mint and two sticks of fresh lemon grass for this recipe.

400g beef rump steak, trimmed
2 small white onions (160g)
2 lebanese cucumbers (260g)
250g cherry tomatoes
1 small fresh red thai chilli, seeded, sliced thinly
¼ cup loosely packed fresh thai basil leaves
¼ cup loosely packed fresh coriander leaves
¼ cup loosely packed fresh vietnamese mint leaves

garlic dressing
2 small fresh red thai chillies, seeded, chopped coarsely
2 tablespoons coarsely chopped fresh lemon grass
⅔ cup loosely packed fresh coriander leaves
3 cloves garlic, quartered
⅓ cup lime juice (80ml)
1 tablespoon fish sauce
1 tablespoon soy sauce

Cook beef on heated oiled grill plate (or grill or barbecue) until browned both sides and cooked as desired. Stand beef, covered, for 5 minutes.

Meanwhile, slice onions thinly. Halve unpeeled cucumbers lengthways; scoop out seeds with a spoon, slice thinly. Halve tomatoes. Combine onion, cucumber, tomato, chilli and herbs in large bowl. Slice beef thinly across the grain; add beef and garlic dressing to bowl, toss salad gently to combine.

garlic dressing Blend or process ingredients until finely chopped.

serves 4
per serving 10.2g fat; 886kJ (212 cal)

marmalade-glazed pork cutlets

½ cup (125ml) dry red wine
⅓ cup (115g) orange marmalade
1 clove garlic, crushed
⅓ cup (80ml) fresh orange juice
1 tablespoon olive oil
4 pork cutlets (940g)

Combine wine, marmalade, garlic and juice in small saucepan; bring to a boil. Remove from heat.
Heat oil in large frying pan; cook pork until browned both sides and cooked as desired, brushing occasionally with marmalade glaze.
Serve with steamed rice and stir-fried baby bok choy or choy sum, if desired.

serves 4
per serving 10.2g fat; 1329kJ (318 cal)

caesar salad

4 slices white bread
4 slices prosciutto (40g)
¼ cup (70g) low-fat yogurt
¼ cup (75g) low-fat mayonnaise
2 cloves garlic, quartered
5 anchovy fillets, drained
½ teaspoon worcestershire sauce
½ teaspoon dijon mustard
1½ tablespoons lemon juice
4 baby cos lettuces
¼ cup (20g) finely grated parmesan cheese

Preheat oven to moderate.
Remove crusts from bread; cut bread into 1cm cubes.
Place on oven tray; bake, uncovered, in moderate oven
about 5 minutes or until croutons are just toasted lightly.
Meanwhile, cook prosciutto, uncovered, stirring, in
medium heated dry non-stick frying pan until browned
and crisp; chop coarsely.
Blend or process yogurt, mayonnaise, garlic, anchovy,
sauce, mustard and juice until almost smooth.
Combine croutons, prosciutto, yogurt mixture, lettuce
leaves and cheese; toss gently to combine.

serves 8
per serving 3.6g fat; 347kJ (83 cal)

stir-fried pork and noodles

*Because the cooking time is so brief in a stir-fry, it's best to use a cut
of meat that doesn't need to be slow-cooked in order to be tender;
we recommend you use thinly sliced pork fillet or rump in this recipe.*

250g fresh egg noodles
2 teaspoons peanut oil
1 clove garlic, crushed
1½ teaspoons five-spice powder
500g pork fillet, sliced thinly
2 small red capsicums (300g), sliced diagonally
2 tablespoons oyster sauce
1 tablespoon soy sauce
1 teaspoon sesame oil
2 teaspoons cornflour
1⅓ cups (330ml) chicken stock
5 green onions, sliced thinly
600g chinese cabbage, finely shredded

Place noodles in large heatproof bowl; cover with boiling water,
stand 3 minutes, using a fork to separate the noodles. Drain into
a colander or large strainer.

Add half of the peanut oil to a heated wok or large frying pan;
stir-fry garlic and five-spice briefly, until just fragrant. Add pork, in
batches, to wok; stir-fry over high heat until browned and almost
cooked through.

Heat remaining peanut oil in wok; stir-fry capsicum for 1 minute.
Return pork to wok; add oyster sauce, soy sauce, sesame oil
and the blended cornflour and chicken stock. Stir-fry over high
heat, tossing, until pork mixture just starts to boil and is thickened
slightly. Add noodles, onion and cabbage to wok; stir-fry over
high heat, tossing to combine, until heated through.

serves 4
per serving 6.7g fat; 1612kJ (385 cal)

thai fish parcels

If you can't buy kaffir lime leaves, substitute the young leaves from any other citrus tree.

200g rice stick noodles
4 x 150g bream fillets
150g baby bok choy, quartered
150g snow peas, sliced thinly lengthways
1 tablespoon thinly sliced lemon grass
8 kaffir lime leaves, torn
1 teaspoon soy sauce
2 tablespoons sweet chilli sauce
1 teaspoon fish sauce
2 tablespoons lime juice
1 tablespoon coarsely chopped fresh coriander

Preheat oven to hot.
Place noodles in large heatproof bowl; cover with boiling water. Stand until just tender; drain.
Divide noodles into four equal portions; place each on a large piece of foil. Top noodles with fish; top fish with equal amounts of bok choy, snow peas, lemon grass and lime leaves. Drizzle with combined sauces and juice. Enclose fish stacks in foil; place in single layer on oven tray.
Cook fish parcels in hot oven 15 minutes or until fish is cooked through; open foil and transfer fish to serving plates. Sprinkle with coriander, serve with noodles.

serves 4
per serving 4.4g fat; 1392kJ (333 cal)
tip Fish parcels can be assembled several hours ahead; store in refrigerator.

salt and pepper scallops with cherry tomato salsa

1kg scallops
2 teaspoons sea salt
½ teaspoon cracked black pepper
2 cloves garlic, crushed
2 teaspoons peanut oil
cherry tomato salsa
400g cherry tomatoes, quartered
2 lebanese cucumbers (260g), seeded, chopped finely
1 medium red onion (170g), chopped finely
4 green onions, sliced thinly
2 tablespoons lemon juice
2 small fresh red thai chillies, seeded, chopped finely

Combine scallops with salt, pepper and garlic in medium bowl; use fingers to sprinkle salt mixture evenly over each scallop. Cover; refrigerate 15 minutes.
Heat oil in wok or large frying pan; stir-fry scallops, in batches, until salt-pepper coating is lightly browned and scallops are cooked as desired. Add scallops to cherry tomato salsa; toss gently to combine.
cherry tomato salsa Combine ingredients in large bowl.

serves 4
per serving 4.3g fat; 815kJ (195 cal)

char-grilled tuna salad

600g tuna steak
¼ cup (60ml) mirin
1 tablespoon light soy sauce
1 clove garlic, crushed
1 small fresh red thai chilli, seeded, chopped finely
1 green onion, chopped finely
2 medium red capsicums (400g), sliced thinly
200g mesclun

Cook tuna on heated oiled grill plate (or grill or barbecue) until browned both sides and cooked as desired. Cover, rest 2 minutes; cut into thick slices.
Meanwhile, combine mirin, soy sauce, garlic, chilli and onion in screw-top jar; shake well.
Combine tuna and dressing in large bowl with capsicum and mesclun; toss gently to combine.

serves 4
per serving 8.9g fat; 1150kJ (275 cal)

crisp-skinned snapper with stir-fried vegetables and black beans

½ teaspoon sea salt

1 teaspoon coarsely
    ground black pepper

4 x 200g snapper fillets

1 teaspoon sesame oil

1 large brown onion (200g),
    cut into thin wedges

1 clove garlic, crushed

1cm piece fresh ginger
    (5g), grated finely

1 tablespoon salted black
    beans, rinsed, drained

1 medium green capsicum
    (200g), chopped coarsely

1 medium red capsicum
    (200g), chopped coarsely

6 green onions,
    sliced thickly

100g snow peas

100g broccolini,
    chopped coarsely

½ cup (125ml) water

¼ cup (60ml) oyster sauce

2 tablespoons lemon juice

500g baby bok choy,
    chopped coarsely

1 cup (80g) bean sprouts

Combine salt and pepper in small bowl; rub into skin side of each fillet. Cook fish, skin-side down, on heated lightly oiled grill plate (or grill or barbecue) until browned and crisp; turn, cook until browned and cooked as desired. Cover to keep warm.

Heat oil in wok or large frying pan; stir-fry brown onion, garlic and ginger until onion softens. Add beans; stir-fry 1 minute. Add capsicums, green onion, snow peas and broccolini; stir-fry until vegetables are just tender.

Stir in the water, sauce and juice; cook, stirring, until mixture thickens slightly. Add bok choy and bean sprouts; stir-fry until heated through. Serve fish on vegetables.

serves 4

per serving 5.3g fat; 1221kJ (292 cal)

tip Broccolini, a cross between broccoli and chinese kale, is milder and sweeter than broccoli. Each long stem is topped by a loose floret that closely resembles broccoli; from floret to stem, broccolini is completely edible. Substitute chinese broccoli (gai larn) for the broccolini in this recipe, if you prefer.

lime and chilli fish baked in banana leaves

2 large banana leaves

4 stalks lemon grass

4 small fresh red thai chillies, seeded, sliced thinly

4 cloves garlic, crushed

1 tablespoon finely grated lime rind

⅓ cup (80ml) lime juice

2cm piece fresh ginger (10g), grated finely

1 cup coarsely chopped fresh coriander

1 cup (250ml) light coconut milk

8 x 150g ling fillets

cooking-oil spray

2 cups (400g) jasmine rice

4 green onions, sliced thinly

Preheat oven to hot.

Trim each banana leaf into four 30cm squares. Using metal tongs, dip one square at a time into large saucepan of boiling water; remove immediately. Rinse under cold running water; pat dry with absorbent paper. Banana leaf squares should be soft and pliable.

Halve lemon grass stalks. Combine chilli, garlic, rind, juice, ginger, coriander and coconut milk in small bowl. Centre each fillet on banana leaf square. Top with lemon grass; drizzle with chilli mixture. Fold square over fish to enclose; secure each parcel with kitchen string.

Place parcels, in single layer, in large baking dish; coat with cooking-oil spray. Roast in hot oven about 10 minutes or until fish is cooked as desired.

Meanwhile, cook rice, uncovered, in large saucepan of boiling water until tender; drain. Stir onion through rice; serve with fish parcels.

serves 8

per serving 7g fat; 1593kJ (381 cal)

tips Foil can be used if banana leaves are unavailable. Banana leaves can be ordered from fruit and vegetable stores. Cut with a sharp knife close to the main stem, then immerse in hot water so leaves will be pliable.

char-grilled polenta cakes with corn salsa

Polenta is made by grinding dried yellow or white corn (maize) kernels to a rough-textured meal.

cooking-oil spray

1 litre (4 cups) water

1 teaspoon salt

1 cup (170g) polenta

2 tablespoons
wholegrain mustard

corn salsa

2 trimmed corn cobs (500g)

1 medium red capsicum
(200g), chopped finely

1 medium red onion
(170g), chopped finely

1 lebanese cucumber
(130g), seeded,
chopped finely

¼ cup coarsely chopped
fresh flat-leaf parsley

1 teaspoon finely
grated lime rind

⅓ cup (80ml) lime juice

2 tablespoons olive oil

3 cloves garlic, crushed

1 tablespoon
sweet chilli sauce

Lightly spray 23cm-square slab cake pan with cooking-oil spray. Bring the water and salt to a boil in large saucepan. Add polenta; cook, stirring, about 10 minutes or until polenta thickens. Add mustard; stir until combined. Spread polenta into slab pan. Cover; refrigerate about 30 minutes or until firm.

Meanwhile, make corn salsa.

Turn polenta onto board; cut into six rectangles. Heat large lightly oiled non-stick frying pan; cook polenta, in batches, until browned both sides. Serve polenta cakes with corn salsa. Top with baby rocket, if desired.

corn salsa Boil, steam or microwave corn until just tender. Drain; cool. Using sharp knife, remove kernels from cob. Combine corn in medium bowl with remaining ingredients.

serves 6

per serving 8.4g fat; 1041kJ (249 cal)

tip You can reduce preparation and cooking times by substituting the fresh corn for a 420g can of corn kernels, drained.

serving suggestion Serve with a salad of rocket or mixed baby greens.

baked spinach and mushroom frittata

1 teaspoon olive oil
3 cloves garlic, crushed
1 small leek (200g),
　sliced thinly
400g button mushrooms,
　sliced thickly
200g baby spinach leaves
2 eggs
6 egg whites
½ cup (125ml) skim milk
⅓ cup (40g) coarsely grated
　low-fat cheddar cheese

Preheat oven to moderately slow.
Oil deep 23cm-round cake pan. Line base with baking paper.
Heat oil in medium frying pan; cook garlic and leek, stirring, until leek softens. Add mushrooms; cook, stirring, until mushrooms are just tender. Add spinach; cook, stirring, until spinach just wilts. Drain off and discard any liquid.
Whisk eggs, egg whites, milk and cheese in large bowl; stir in vegetable mixture.
Pour egg mixture into prepared pan. Bake in moderately slow oven about 30 minutes or until just set. Place frittata under hot grill until browned. Top with baby spinach, if desired.

serves 4
per serving 5.3g fat; 602kJ (144 cal)
tip Use swiss brown mushrooms as an alternative tasty mushroom.

rice noodle salad

You will need about half a medium red cabbage for this recipe.

150g rice stick noodles
¼ cup (60ml) lime juice
¼ cup (60ml) sweet chilli sauce
1 tablespoon light soy sauce
1 tablespoon sugar
6 cups (480g) finely shredded red cabbage
1 large carrot (180g), sliced thinly
1 lebanese cucumber (130g), seeded, sliced thinly
3 medium egg tomatoes (225g), seeded, sliced thinly
1 medium yellow capsicum (200g), sliced thinly
½ cup firmly packed fresh coriander leaves
½ cup firmly packed fresh mint leaves
½ cup firmly packed fresh thai basil leaves

Place noodles in large heatproof bowl; cover with boiling water. Stand until just tender; drain.
Meanwhile, combine juice, sauces and sugar in small bowl; stir until sugar dissolves.
Place noodles in large bowl with juice mixture and remaining ingredients; toss to combine.

serves 4
per serving 1.6g fat; 903kJ (216 cal)
tips Rice stick noodles and dried rice noodles are virtually the same thing, however, rice stick noodles are thicker. The two can easily be interchanged in recipes.

tofu cakes with sweet chilli dipping sauce

You need to cook about ⅓ cup basmati rice for this recipe.

300g fresh firm tofu

1 cup (150g) cooked
    basmati rice

3 teaspoons
    red curry paste

2 green onions,
    chopped finely

1 tablespoon coarsely
    chopped fresh coriander

1 egg, beaten lightly

sweet chilli dipping sauce

¼ cup (60ml) white vinegar

½ cup (110g) caster sugar

½ teaspoon salt

¾ cup (180ml) water

½ small red onion (50g),
    chopped finely

½ small carrot (35g),
    chopped finely

½ small lebanese
    cucumber (65g),
    seeded, chopped finely

2 tablespoons coarsely
    chopped fresh coriander

⅓ cup (80ml)
    sweet chilli sauce

Press tofu between two chopping boards or trays, place weight on top; elevate boards slightly to allow tofu liquid to drain away. Stand 20 minutes; chop coarsely. Blend or process tofu until smooth.

Preheat oven to moderately hot; line oven tray with baking paper.

Combine tofu in medium bowl with rice, paste, onion, coriander and egg.

Shape level tablespoons of the tofu mixture into rounds; place on oven tray, press lightly with fork to flatten.

Bake, uncovered, in moderately hot oven, about 10 minutes or until lightly browned and heated through. Serve tofu cakes with sweet chilli dipping sauce.

sweet chilli dipping sauce Place vinegar, sugar, salt and the water in small saucepan; bring to a boil. Boil, stirring, about 2 minutes or until sugar dissolves. Pour vinegar mixture over remaining ingredients in medium heatproof bowl; stir to combine.

makes 20 tofu cakes

per cake 1.7g fat; 326kJ (78 cal)

white bean salad with coriander, mint and lemon grass

2 x 400g cans cannellini beans, rinsed, drained
150g baby spinach leaves
1 small red onion (100g), sliced thinly
1 clove garlic, crushed
1 tablespoon coarsely chopped fresh coriander
1 tablespoon coarsely chopped fresh mint
1 tablespoon thinly sliced fresh lemon grass
1cm piece fresh ginger (5g), grated finely
2 tablespoons sesame oil
2 tablespoons soy sauce
2 tablespoons sweet chilli sauce
2 tablespoons lime juice
1 teaspoon honey
2 small fresh red thai chillies, seeded, sliced thinly

Combine beans in large bowl with spinach and onion.
Combine garlic, herbs, lemon grass, ginger, oil,
sauces, juice and honey in screw-top jar; shake well.
Just before serving, drizzle dressing over salad; toss
gently to combine, then sprinkle with chilli.

serves 4
per serving 10.1g fat; 698kJ (197 cal)

pumpkin gnocchi

16 medium egg tomatoes (1.2kg), quartered
1.6kg butternut pumpkin
1 egg
2 tablespoons finely chopped fresh flat-leaf parsley
2 tablespoons finely chopped fresh basil
2 cups (300g) plain flour
1 cup (150g) self-raising flour
2 teaspoons olive oil
1 small leek (200g), sliced thinly
1.5kg spinach, chopped coarsely
2 tablespoons olive paste
½ cup (40g) flaked parmesan cheese

Preheat oven to hot.
Place tomato in large non-stick baking dish; bake, uncovered, in hot oven about 20 minutes or until browned lightly and softened.
Meanwhile, peel pumpkin; chop coarsely. Boil, steam or microwave until tender; drain. Blend or process cooled pumpkin and egg until smooth; place in large bowl. Using hand, mix in herbs and flours. Turn pumpkin dough onto floured surface; knead lightly for about 2 minutes or until smooth. Roll heaped teaspoons of dough into gnocchi-shaped ovals; press lightly against back of fork tines. Place gnocchi on tray. Cover; refrigerate 30 minutes.
Heat oil in large non-stick frying pan; cook leek, stirring, until softened. Add spinach; cook, stirring, until spinach is just wilted.
Cook gnocchi, uncovered, in large saucepan of boiling water until all gnocchi float to surface. Carefully remove gnocchi from pan using slotted spoon; drain. Serve gnocchi on spinach-leek mixture; top with tomato, olive paste and cheese.

serves 8
per serving 5.7g fat; 1438kJ (344 cal)

pasta with fresh tomato sauce

This is a great short-order dish that can be prepared in about the time it
takes to warm the bread and open the wine.

375g fresh lasagne sheets, sliced thickly
1 tablespoon extra virgin olive oil
6 medium tomatoes (900g), peeled, seeded, chopped coarsely
¼ cup coarsely chopped fresh basil
2 cloves garlic, crushed
2 teaspoons red wine vinegar
1 small fresh red thai chilli, seeded, chopped finely
80g low-fat fetta cheese, crumbled

Cook pasta in large saucepan of boiling water, uncovered,
until just tender; drain. Sprinkle half of the oil over pasta; toss
gently to combine.
Combine tomato, basil, garlic, remaining oil, vinegar and
chilli in medium bowl.
Divide pasta among serving plates. Spoon tomato mixture
over pasta; sprinkle with cheese.

serves 4
per serving 8.8g fat; 1852kJ (443 cal)
tips To peel tomatoes, slice a cross in the bottom of tomato.
Place tomatoes in large bowl of boiling water for 1 minute;
drain. Rinse under cold water; peel.
Fresh lasagne sheets, available loose by weight from good
delis or in cryovac packages from supermarkets, take virtually
no time at all to cook.

51

strawberry smoothie

200g low-fat frozen strawberry yogurt
250g strawberries
1 litre (4 cups) skim milk

Soften yogurt slightly, cut into pieces. Hull
strawberries, cut each in half. Blend or process
all ingredients, in batches, until smooth.

serves 4
per serving 3.5g fat; 782kJ (187 cal)

peach smoothie

2 cups (500ml) no-fat soy milk
2 medium bananas (400g), chopped coarsely
4 medium peaches (600g), chopped coarsely
½ teaspoon ground cinnamon

Blend or process ingredients, in batches, until smooth.

serves 4
per serving 0.9g fat; 635kJ (152 cal)

mocha self-saucing pudding

Originally the name of a Middle-Eastern seaport from which premium arabic coffee was exported, the word mocha has evolved to describe the serendipitous combination of coffee and chocolate.

1 cup (150g) self-raising flour
⅓ cup (35g) cocoa powder
¾ cup (165g) caster sugar
2½ teaspoons instant coffee powder
½ cup (125ml) skim milk
1 tablespoon vegetable oil
½ cup (100g) firmly packed brown sugar
1¼ cups (310ml) boiling water
1 tablespoon icing sugar mixture

Preheat oven to moderately slow.

Sift flour, 2 tablespoons of the cocoa, sugar and 2 teaspoons of the coffee powder into 1.25-litre (5-cup) ovenproof dish; gradually stir in milk and oil.

Sift brown sugar, remaining cocoa and remaining coffee evenly over flour mixture; gently pour the water over brown sugar mixture.

Bake pudding, uncovered, in moderately slow oven about 45 minutes; serve dusted with sifted icing sugar.

serves 4

per serving 6.3g fat; 2073kJ (496 cal)

tip This pudding is best served hot because the sauce is quickly absorbed by the pudding.

apple and fig bread pudding

Granny Smith and Golden Delicious are the best apple varieties to use for this recipe.

2 tablespoons honey
2 tablespoons water
8 slices white bread
1 medium apple (150g), cored, quartered, sliced thinly
12 dried figs (200g), halved
2 cups (500ml) skim milk
2 eggs
2 tablespoons caster sugar
½ teaspoon ground cinnamon
2 teaspoons icing sugar mixture

Preheat oven to moderately slow.

Stir honey and the water in small saucepan over low heat until honey melts.

Cut crusts from bread; discard crusts. Halve slices diagonally; brush both sides of bread with honey mixture. Layer bread, apple and fig, overlapping pieces slightly, in lightly greased shallow rectangular 1.25-litre (5 cup) ovenproof dish.

Whisk milk, eggs and sugar together in medium bowl; strain into large jug, skimming and discarding any foam. Pour half the milk mixture over the bread; stand 5 minutes. Pour over remaining milk mixture; sprinkle with cinnamon.

Place dish in large baking dish; add enough boiling water to come halfway up sides of dish. Bake pudding, uncovered, in moderately slow oven about 45 minutes or until top is browned lightly and pudding is set. Dust with sifted icing sugar before serving.

serves 4

per serving 3g fat; 1185kJ (283 cal)

tip Remove bread and butter pudding from water bath immediately after cooking to prevent it from overcooking and becoming tough.

passionfruit soufflés

You need four large passionfruit for this recipe.

1 tablespoon caster sugar
2 egg yolks
⅓ cup (80ml) fresh passionfruit pulp
2 tablespoons Cointreau
½ cup (80g) icing sugar mixture
4 egg whites
2 teaspoons icing sugar mixture, extra

Preheat oven to moderate.
Lightly grease four 1-cup (250ml) ovenproof dishes.
Sprinkle insides of dishes evenly with caster sugar; shake
away excess. Place dishes on oven tray.
Whisk yolks, passionfruit pulp, liqueur and 2 tablespoons
of the icing sugar in large bowl until mixture is combined.
Beat egg whites in small bowl with electric mixer until soft
peaks form. Gradually add remaining icing sugar; beat until
firm peaks form. Gently fold egg white mixture, in two
batches, into passionfruit mixture; divide mixture among
prepared dishes.
Bake, uncovered, in moderate oven about 12 minutes or
until soufflés are puffed and browned lightly. Dust tops with
extra sifted icing sugar; serve immediately.

serves 4
per serving 2.9g fat; 886kJ (212 cal)

glossary

bamboo shoot tender shoots of bamboo plants, available in cans; must be drained and rinsed before use.

bean sprouts also known as bean shoots; tender new growths of assorted beans and seeds germinated for consumption as sprouts.

bok choy also called pak choi or chinese white cabbage; has a fresh, mild mustard taste, and is good braised or in stir-fries. Baby bok choy is also available, and is slightly more tender than bok choy.

broccolini a cross between broccoli and chinese kale, is milder and sweeter than broccoli. Each long stem is topped by a loose floret that closely resembles broccoli; from floret to stem, broccolini is completely edible.

cabbage, chinese also known as peking or napa cabbage, wong bok and petsai. Elongated in shape with pale green, crinkly leaves. This is the most common cabbage in South-East Asia.

cannellini beans small, dried white bean similar in flavour and appearance to great northern, navy or haricot bean.

capsicum also known as bell pepper or, simply, pepper. Discard seeds and membranes before use.

chickpeas also known as hummus, garbanzos or channa; an irregularly round, sandy-coloured legume.

cocoa powder also known as cocoa; unsweetened cocoa beans are dried, roasted, then ground.

cointreau citrus-flavoured liqueur; a blend of fragrant peels from both bitter and sweet oranges.

coriander also known as pak chee, cilantro or chinese parsley; bright-green-leafed herb with a pungent flavour.

cornflour also known as cornstarch; used as a thickening agent in cooking.

egg noodles, fresh, also known as ba mee or yellow noodles; made from wheat flour and eggs. Range in size from very fine strands to wide, thick spaghetti-like pieces as thick as a shoelace.

fish sauce also called nam pla or nuoc nam; made from pulverized, salted, fermented fish, most often anchovies. Has a pungent smell and strong taste; there are many versions of varying intensity, so use according to your taste.

five-spice powder a fragrant mixture of ground cinnamon, cloves, star anise, sichuan pepper and fennel seeds.

flour

plain: an all-purpose flour, made from wheat.

self-raising: plain flour sifted with baking powder in the proportion of 1 cup flour to 2 teaspoons baking powder.

ginger, fresh also known as green or root ginger; the thick gnarled root of a tropical plant.

kaffir lime leaves aromatic leaves of a small citrus tree; used similarly to bay leaves or curry leaves.

kecap manis also known as ketjap manis. A thick soy sauce with added sugar and spices.

lebanese cucumber long, slender and thin-skinned; is also known as the european or burpless cucumber.

lemon grass a tall, clumping, lemon-smelling and -tasting, sharp-edged grass; the white lower part of the stem is used, finely chopped, in cooking.

marmalade a preserve, usually based on citrus fruit.

mayonnaise, low-fat, we used cholesterol-free mayonnaise with 3% fat content.

mesclun a mixture of assorted young lettuce and other green leaves; also sold as salad mix or gourmet salad mix.

mince meat also known as ground meat, as in beef, pork, lamb, chicken and veal.

mirin sweet rice wine used in Japanese cooking; not to be confused with sake.

mushroom

button: small, cultivated white mushrooms with a mild flavour.

oyster: also known as abalone; grey-white mushroom shaped like a fan. Smooth texture with subtle, oyster-like flavour.

mustard

dijon: pale brown, distinctively flavoured, mild french mustard.

wholegrain: also known as seeded. A French-style coarse-grain mustard made from crushed mustard seeds and dijon-style french mustard.

oil

olive: made from ripened olives; extra virgin and virgin are the best. Extra light or light refers to taste not fat levels.

peanut: pressed from ground peanuts; commonly used oil in Asian cooking because of its high smoke point (handles high heat without burning).

sesame: made from roasted, crushed, white sesame seeds.

vegetable: any of a number of oils sourced from plants rather than animal fats.

onion

green: also known as scallion or, incorrectly, shallot; an immature onion picked before the bulb has formed, having a long, bright-green edible stalk.

red: also known as spanish, red spanish or bermuda onion; a sweet-flavoured, large, purple-red onion.

oyster sauce made from oysters and their brine; cooked with salt and soy sauce, and thickened with starches.

paprika, ground, dried red capsicum (bell pepper); available sweet or hot.

polenta a flour-like cereal made of ground corn (maize); similar to cornmeal.

rice noodles, fresh can be purchased in various widths or large sheets, which are cut into the noodle width desired. Chewy and pure white; they do not need pre-cooking before use.

rice paper sheets also known as banh trang. Made from rice paste and stamped into rounds. Quite brittle, and will break if dropped. Dipped momentarily in water to become a pliable wrapper for vegetables.

rice stick noodles also known as sen lek, ho fun or kway teow; dried noodles made from rice flour and water. Available in different widths; soak in hot water until soft.

rice

basmati: fragrant, long-grained white rice. Wash several times before cooking.

jasmine: fragrant, long-grained rice; can substitute with white rice, but taste will be different.

sambal oelek (also ulek or olek) Indonesian in origin; a salty paste made from ground chillies and vinegar.

skim milk we used milk with 0.1% fat content.

snow peas also known as mange tout ("eat all"). Snow pea tendrils are the growing shoots of the plant.

soy sauce also known as sieu, is made from fermented soy beans. Several variations are available, we used a mild Japanese variety.

spinach also known as english spinach and, incorrectly, silverbeet.

stock stock cubes, powder or concentrated liquid can be used. As a guide, 1 teaspoon of stock powder or 1 small crumbled stock cube or 1 portion stock concentrate mixed with 1 cup (250ml) water will give a fairly strong stock. Be aware of the salt and fat content of stocks.

sugar we used coarse, granulated table sugar, also known as crystal sugar, unless otherwise specified.

brown: an extremely soft, fine granulated sugar retaining molasses for its characteristic colour and flavour.

caster: also known as superfine or finely granulated table sugar.

icing sugar mixture: also known as confectioners'

sugar or powdered sugar.

palm: also known as nam tan pip, jaggery, jawa or gula melaka; made from the sap of the sugar palm tree. Light brown to black in colour, and usually sold in rock-hard cakes; substitute it with brown sugar if unavailable.

sweet chilli sauce the comparatively mild, thin thai sauce made from red chillies, sugar, garlic and vinegar; used as a condiment more often than in cooking.

thai basil also known as horapa; has small, crinkly leaves with strong, somewhat bitter, flavour. Available from Asian supermarkets.

thai chilli bright red to dark green in colour, ranging in size from small ("scuds") to long and thin; among the hottest of chillies.

tofu also known as bean curd, an off-white, custard-like product made from the "milk" of crushed soy beans; comes fresh as soft or firm. Leftover fresh tofu can be refrigerated in water (which is changed daily) up to 4 days.

tortillas thin, round unleavened bread originating in Mexico. Two kinds are available, one made from wheat flour and the other from corn.

vinegar

cider: made from fermented apples; has a strong taste.

white: made from spirit of cane sugar.

worcestershire sauce a thin, dark-brown, spicy sauce used as a seasoning for meat and gravies, and as a condiment.

index

These conversions are approximate only, but the difference between an exact and the approximate conversion of various liquid and dry measures is minimal and will not affect your cooking results.

Measuring equipment

The difference between one country's measuring cups and another's is, at most, within a 2 or 3 teaspoon variance. (For the record, 1 Australian metric measuring cup holds approximately 250ml.) The most accurate way of measuring dry ingredients is to weigh them. For liquids, use a clear glass or plastic jug having metric markings.

Note: NZ, Canada, US and UK all use 15ml tablespoons. Australian tablespoons measure 20ml. All cup and spoon measurements are level.

How to measure

When using graduated measuring cups, shake dry ingredients loosely into the appropriate cup. Do not tap the cup on a bench or tightly pack the ingredients unless directed to do so. Level the top of measuring cups and measuring spoons with a knife. When measuring liquids, place a clear glass or plastic jug having metric markings on a flat surface to check accuracy at eye level.

Dry measures

metric	imperial
15g	½oz
30g	1oz
60g	2oz
90g	3oz
125g	4oz (¼lb)
155g	5oz
185g	6oz
220g	7oz
250g	8oz (½lb)
280g	9oz
315g	10oz
345g	11oz
375g	12oz (¾lb)
410g	13oz
440g	14oz
470g	15oz
500g	16oz (1lb)
750g	24oz (1½lb)
1kg	32oz (2lb)

We use large eggs with an average weight of 60g.

Liquid measures

metric	imperial
30 ml	1 fluid oz
60 ml	2 fluid oz
100 ml	3 fluid oz
125 ml	4 fluid oz
150 ml	5 fluid oz (¼ pint/1 gill)
190 ml	6 fluid oz
250 ml (1cup)	8 fluid oz
300 ml	10 fluid oz (½ pint)
500 ml	16 fluid oz
600 ml	20 fluid oz (1 pint)
1000 ml (1litre)	1¾ pints

Helpful measures

metric	imperial
3mm	⅛in
6mm	¼in
1cm	½in
2cm	¾in
2.5cm	1in
6cm	2½in
8cm	3in
20cm	8in
23cm	9in
25cm	10in
30cm	12in (1ft)

Oven temperatures

These oven temperatures are only a guide.
Always check the manufacturer's manual.

	°C (Celsius)	°F (Fahrenheit)	Gas Mark
Very slow	120	250	½
Slow	140 – 150	275 – 300	1 – 2
Moderately slow	170	325	3
Moderate	180 –190	350 – 375	4 – 5
Moderately hot	200	400	6
Hot	220 – 230	425 – 450	7 – 8
Very hot	240	475	9

at your fingertips

These elegant bookcovers store up to 10 mini books and make the books instantly accessible.

And the metric measuring cups and spoons make following our recipes a piece of cake.

Book Holder
Australia and overseas:
$8.95 (incl. GST).

Metric Measuring Set
Australia: $6.50 (incl. GST).
New Zealand: $8.00.
Elsewhere: $9.95.
Prices include postage and handling. This offer is available in all countries.

Photocopy and complete coupon below

Mail or fax Photocopy and complete the coupon below and post to
ACP Books Reader Offer,
ACP Books, GPO Box 4967,
Sydney NSW 2001, *or* fax to (02) 9267 4967.

Phone Have your credit card details ready, then phone 136 116 (Mon-Fri, 8.00am-6.00pm; Sat, 8.00am-6.00pm).

Australian residents We accept the credit cards listed on the coupon, money orders and cheques.

Overseas residents We accept the credit cards listed on the coupon, drafts in $A drawn on an Australian bank, and also UK, NZ and US cheques in the currency of the country of issue. Credit card charges are at the exchange rate current at the time of payment.

☐ **Book Holder**   ☐ **Metric Measuring Set**
Please indicate number(s) required.

Mr/Mrs/Ms _____

Address _____

_____

Postcode _____ Country _____

Ph: Business hours ( ) _____

I enclose my cheque/money order for $ _____ payable to ACP Publishing.

OR: please charge $ _____ to my ☐ Bankcard ☐ Mastercard

☐ Visa ☐ American Express ☐ Diners Club

Expiry date ____ /____

Card number

Cardholder's signature _____

Please allow up to 30 days delivery within Australia.
Allow up to 6 weeks for overseas deliveries.
Both offers expire 31/12/05. HLMSF05

Food director Pamela Clark
Food editor Louise Patniotis
Nutritional information Laila Ibram
ACP BOOKS
Editorial director Susan Tomnay
Creative director Hieu Chi Nguyen
Senior editor Wendy Bryant
Designer Mary Keep
Assistant designer Josii Do
Editorial coordinator Merryn Pearse
Sales director Brian Cearnes
Rights manager Jane Hazell
Brand manager Renée Crea
Marketing director Matt Dominello
Sales & marketing coordinator Gabrielle Botto
Pre-press by Harry Palmer
Production manager Carol Currie
Chief executive officer John Alexander
Group publisher Pat Ingram
Publisher Sue Wannan
Editor-in-chief Deborah Thomas
Produced by ACP Books, Sydney.
Printing by Dai Nippon Printing in Korea.
Published by ACP Publishing Pty Limited,
54 Park St, Sydney;
GPO Box 4088, Sydney, NSW 2001.
Ph: (02) 9282 8618 Fax: (02) 9267 9438.
acpbooks@acp.com.au
www.acpbooks.com.au
To order books phone 136 116.
Send recipe enquiries to
Recipeenquiries@acp.com.au
Australia Distributed by Network Services,
GPO Box 4088, Sydney, NSW 2001.
Ph: (02) 9282 8777 Fax: (02) 9264 3278.
United Kingdom Distributed by Australian
Consolidated Press (UK), Moulton Park Business
Centre, Red House Road, Moulton Park,
Northampton, NN3 6AQ. Ph: (01604) 497 531
Fax: (01604) 497 533 acpukltd@aol.com
Canada Distributed by Whitecap Books Ltd,
351 Lynn Ave, North Vancouver, BC, V7J 2C4,
Ph: (604) 980 9852 Fax: (604) 980 8197
customerservice@whitecap.ca
www.whitecap.ca
New Zealand Distributed by Netlink Distribution
Company, ACP Media Centre, Cnr Fanshawe
and Beaumont Streets, Westhaven, Auckland;
PO Box 47906, Ponsonby, Auckland, NZ.
Ph: (09) 366 9966 ask@ndcnz.co.nz
South Africa Distributed by PSD Promotions,
30 Diesel Road, Isando, Gauteng, Johannesbur
PO Box 1175, Isando, 1600, Gauteng, Johannes
Ph (27 11) 392 6065/7 Fax: (27 11) 392 6079/80
orders@psdprom.co.za

Clark, Pamela.
The Australian Women's Weekly
Skinny Food.
Includes index.
ISBN 1 86396 355 3
1. Low-calorie diet – Recipes. 2. Low-fat diet –
Recipes. I. Title. II. Title: Skinny food.
III. Title: Australian Women's Weekly.
641.5635
© ACP Publishing Pty Limited 2004
ABN 18 053 273 546
First published 2004. Reprinted 2004, 2005 (twi
Cover Passionfruit soufflés, page 59.
Stylist Julz Beresford
Photographer Ben Dearnley
Home economist Susie Riggall
Back cover at left, Stir-fried pork and noodles,
page 27; at right, Lamb chermoulla with chickpe
salad, page 16.